## GUARDING

# THE FEDERAL RESERVE BANK OF NEW YORK

BY PEGGY CARAVANTES

Published by The Child's World®
1980 Lookout Drive • Mankato, MN 56003-1705
800-599-READ • www.childsworld.com

Acknowledgments
The Child's World®: Mary Swensen, Publishing Director
Red Line Editorial: Editorial direction and production
The Design Lab: Design

Design Element: Iaroslav Neliubov/Shutterstock Images
Photographs ©: Shutterstock Images, cover, 1; Randy Olson/National Geographic Creative/Corbis, 5, 7, 11; R. Babakin/Shutterstock Images, 8; Bettmann/Corbis, 13; NYHS/Splash News/Corbis, 14; Mike Segar/Reuters, 17; A. M. Ahad/AP Images, 18; Ramin Talaie/Corbis, 20



ISBN 9781503808119
LCCN 2015958272

Printed in the United States of America
Mankato, MN
June, 2016
PA02302

## ABOUT THE AUTHOR

Peggy Caravantes is the award-winning author of more than 20 middle grade and young adult biographies and children's history books. She is a retired educator and mother to three adult children. Active with church volunteer work, Caravantes also serves as a Reading Buddy tutor in a local elementary school. She resides in San Antonio, Texas.

# TABLE OF CONTENTS

# CHAPTER 1

# Lots of Gold

Millions of people walk around New York City each day. Many do not know they are traveling above a huge collection of gold. It is in a **vault** 80 feet (24.4 m) below 33 Liberty Street. It is part of the Federal Reserve Bank.

The vault is half the size of a football field and rests on New York's bottom layer of rock. That was the only place strong enough to hold the vault. Solid rock also surrounds the vault on all sides. It rests under three stories of other stacked vaults. Its 10-foot (3 m) thick walls are made of concrete. The vault is **reinforced** by steel rods. There are no ordinary doors into it.

The vault's gold is not owned by one person. Much of it belongs to 48 foreign countries and 12 worldwide groups. The United States owns only about 5 percent of it. Most of the rest of the country's gold is stored in Fort Knox, Kentucky, and West Point,

Gold bars sit stacked in the vault of the Federal Reserve Bank of New York.

New York. The Federal Reserve Bank of New York does not charge for guarding and storing gold. It costs $1.75 per bar to move it within or ship it out of the vault for trade or sale. There are somewhere between 500,000 and 550,000 bars in the bank.

Countries like having their gold in New York. It is a major financial city. The location is great for trading and buying gold. The bank protects the gold and keeps detailed records. This gives users peace of mind. They know their valuable gold is safe.

Most of the gold is in bar-shaped bricks. A bar weighs about 27 pounds (12.2 kg). However, the bricks are not pure gold. Each bar has small amounts of some other metal. This can be copper, silver, iron, or platinum. The bars would be too soft to move and store if they were pure gold.

A bar's appearance provides hints about its history. A slight tinge to the brick's color is the first clue. It shows the kind of metal added to make the gold stronger. Silver and platinum

**HERSHEY BARS**

**Some of the vault's gold bars are smaller than others. Melted gold might be left over at the end of casting. Sometimes there is not enough to make a regular brick. So the leftovers are shaped into a smaller one. It is called a Hershey bar. These are pure gold.**

## MOVING THE GOLD

give the gold a whitish shade. Copper provides a red tint. Iron makes it look a bit greenish blue.

The bar's shape tells where it was molded. Bars made in the United States used to be shaped like

The cornerstone of the Federal Reserve Bank of New York's current location was laid on May 31, 1922.

rectangular bricks. They were 7 inches (17.8 cm) long, 3.625 inches (9.2 cm) wide, and between 1.625 (4.1 cm) and 1.75 inches (4.4 cm) thick. Now, each U.S. molding city changes the shape just a little. Denver bars have rounded sides. San Francisco rounds the corners. New York prefers square edges. The United States also now casts **trapezoid** bars. This makes it easier to remove them from the mold.

### THE BUILDING

The Federal Reserve Bank of New York was completed in 1924. It was built on part of a Dutch farm. Many structures were torn down to make room for the bank. It was the largest bank building in the world at that time. The 22-story bank now covers an entire city block. Inset bronze doors and windows make it look like a fort.

The gold bars are moved in a pattern. They are stacked on wooden **pallets**. The bars are placed one at a time. They overlap similar to the way bricks are placed in a wall. Lifting and moving the gold bars is hard work. Gold stackers need rest. They work in shifts. They must be careful not to drop a bar on their foot. They wear steel-toed boots and lightweight magnesium shoe covers for protection. That gear is just part of the security measures used to guard so much valuable gold.

# CHAPTER 2

# Tight Security

There are no chances taken when it comes to protecting gold. Tight security begins when pallets arrive at the dock. They are transported in an armored car. Bullets and even hand grenades cannot stop these trucks.

A pallet is loaded into a security elevator. The pallet is sent to the vault five floors below the street. Armed guards stay with the gold at all times. Everyone is quiet. An operator in a distant room controls the elevators. He talks to the guards through an **intercom**.

The guards and the gold go through an unusual system to enter the vault. The main door of the vault is a 90-ton (81,646 kg), 9-foot (2.7 m) steel **cylinder**. It rotates in a 140-ton (127,006 kg) steel and concrete frame. A 10-foot (3 m) long narrow passage cuts through the center of the cylinder. This becomes the entrance into the vault when it is parallel to the

A control group helps deliver gold to the vault at the Federal Reserve Bank of New York in 2008.

frame. A handwheel turns the cylinder. It rotates 90 degrees each time it moves. This movement either opens or closes the entrance to the vault.

A second handwheel pushes the tapered cylinder .375 inch (.95 cm) into the frame. This forms an airtight seal. It has the same effect as pushing a cork into a bottle. Four steel rods are set back inside the cylinder. Two **levers** can move these bolts into holes. This stops the cylinder completely.

A control group keeps the gold safe inside the vault. The members of this group come from three bank departments. These are **auditing**, vault services, and protection. All three must be present whenever gold is moved into, out of, or within the vault.

The control group checks and weighs the gold. Each bar has four distinct markings on it. They signify the year cast, purity, maker, and serial number of the bar. Weight and purity are what decide a bar's value. A power hoist is used to lift gold onto an old-fashioned scale. It weighed the gold to the nearest .001 ounce (.03 g). That is about one-third the weight of a dollar bill. Today, a more exact, modern electronic scale is used.

The control group checks the information. Bars are then moved to one of 122 **compartments**. These are assigned to the gold's owners. Each compartment has three locks and an auditor's

A man weighs gold bars on an old scale at the Federal Reserve Bank of New York in 1973.

signed paper seal. The locks have several controls. No one person has the numbers to all of them.

A small compartment holds about 6,000 bars. The largest has 107,000 bars. Those bars are stacked to

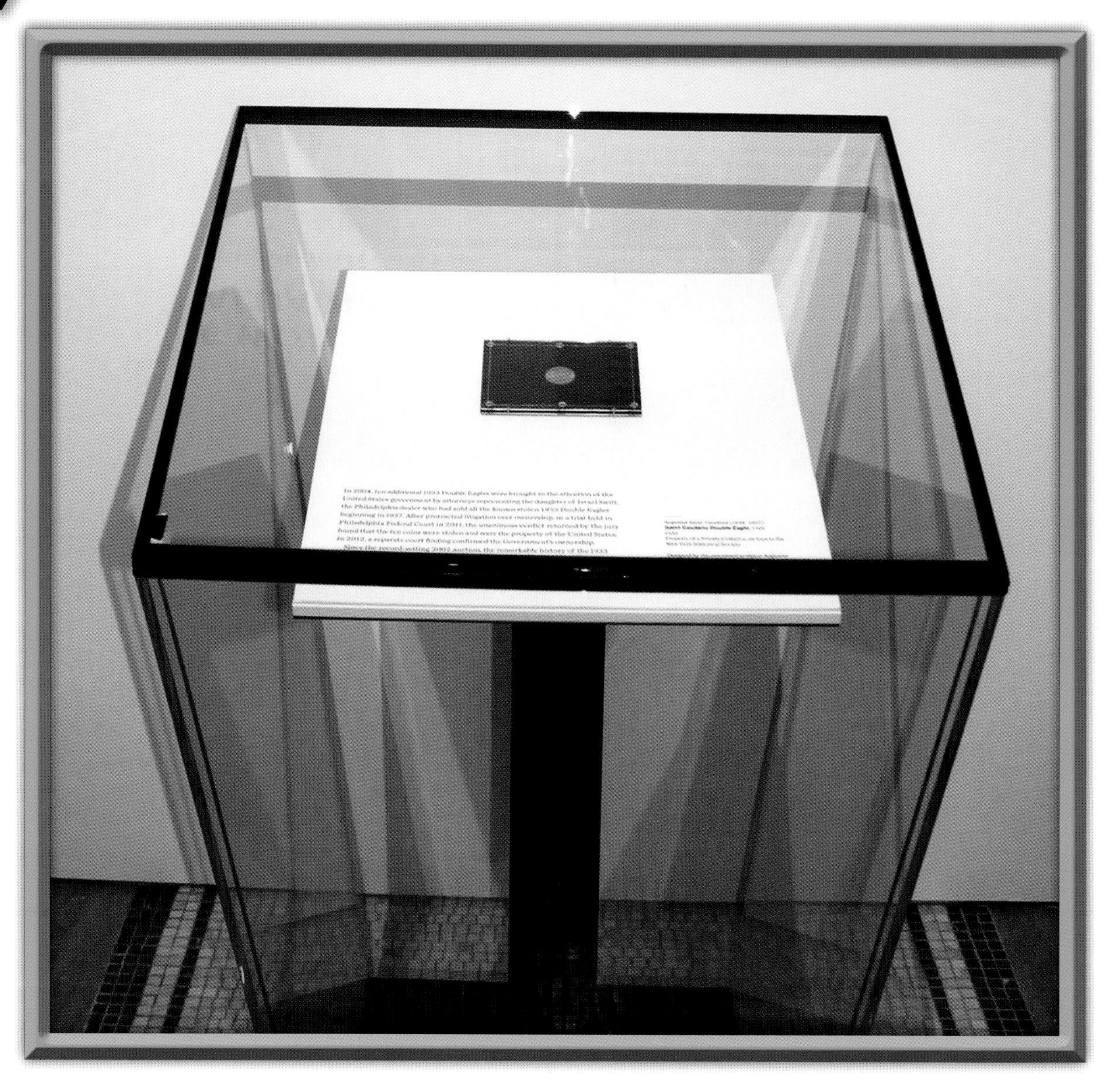

One of the only things known about this 1933 double eagle gold coin is that it is worth almost $7.6 million.

form part of the vault's display for visitors. The bricks make a gold wall. It is 10 feet (3 m) high, 10 feet (3 m) wide, and 18 feet (5.5 m) deep. The value of the bars in the wall is about $17.1 billion. However, gold's exact value changes every day.

All the vault's gold together is valued at about $200 billion. The value changes based on varying rates. Armed guards in uniform help protect it. Guards and other Federal Reserve Bank employees must pass a background check to get a job. To keep their jobs, guards must take a shooting test twice a year. The bank has its own firing range. The guards have to score at least as "marksmen" with three different guns. Most rate "expert."

**THE GOLD DOUBLE EAGLE**

**In 2002, a rare 1933 $20 double eagle gold coin was auctioned for $7,590,020. That made it the world's most valuable coin. The buyer's identity is still a secret. The coin used to be held in the New York vault. But that changed in August 2013. The coin was moved to the New York Historical Society. It is on display there.**

TVs and a **surveillance** system watch all activity. They alert guards anytime someone enters or leaves the vault. All security areas and bank exits can be shut down in less than 25 seconds if an alarm sounds.

# CHAPTER 3

# Protecting the Bank

Perhaps the Federal Reserve Bank's tightest security was on hand when the bank opened its doors in 1924. Forty-five armored cars brought the first gold to the vault. One hundred fifty policemen protected the route. Men with rifles stood on roofs overlooking the street. More than 700 tons (1.4 million pounds) of gold, silver, and paper money were moved to the vault that day.

The Federal Reserve Bank went into lockdown during the September 11, 2001, attacks. Terrorists crashed planes into towers of the nearby World Trade Center. The bank was locked down again a few years later. Gunshots were heard coming from Wall Street. It is two blocks away from the bank. Neither of these incidents were directed at the Federal Reserve Bank.

A police officer stands guard outside the Federal Reserve Bank of New York on September 17, 2001, the day the building reopened after the September 11 terrorist attacks.

In 2012, a 21-year-old man tried to bomb the New York Federal Reserve Bank. Quazi Nafis was from Bangladesh. He first came to the United States to study. However, he later revealed his real purpose.

Quazi Nafis's father holds a photo of Nafis, who was sentenced to prison after his bombing hoax at the Federal Reserve Bank of New York.

He wanted to build a 1,000-pound (453.6 kg) bomb. He reached out for help on social media. The man who responded was a government informant.

He told a secret agent. Nafis did not know that. The agent pretended to help the young terrorist build a bomb. Of course, it was fake. But Nafis thought it was real.

Nafis scouted the Federal Reserve Building. He took pictures to help decide where to put the bomb. Federal agents took pictures of him doing this.

Nafis put the bomb in a van. He parked it near the bank's door. Then he went to a nearby hotel. At 8 a.m. on October 12, 2012, he picked up his cell phone. He dialed the number meant to make the bomb explode. Nothing happened. He tried again and again. Agents arrested Nafis when they were sure he had made the call.

No one in the bank was in danger. The explosives were all fake. But a real bomb of that size could have destroyed the building. It could have killed hundreds of people. Nafis was sentenced to 30 years in prison.

William Dudley became the president and CEO of the Federal Reserve Bank of New York in 2009.

Gold can capture the attention of people around the world. The bank's strong security does not keep tourists from seeing its treasure. Free one-hour tours are given five days a week. They feature groups of 25. About 180 people tour the bank per day. Visitors must be at least 16 years old. They have to go through a long security check. Then a visitor receives a ticket. It must be shown with a government-issued identification to enter the vault. No phones or cameras are allowed.

**THE IMPORTANCE OF GOLD**

Currency varies around the world. But gold is constant. There are a few reasons for this. One is that it does not break down physically. Another is that it does not vary in quality. This means all gold can be valued the same. Finally, there is a limited amount of gold in the world. That means people cannot just find more. This also helps bring stable value.

Despite the many tours, no one has ever tried to rob the vault. Even if they did, they would have quite a lot of trouble getting through all the tough security in place.

## GLOSSARY

**auditing (AW-dit-ing)** Auditing is making sure financial records are correct. Auditing is the responsibility of the control group in the gold vault.

**compartments (kuhm-PAHRT-muhnts)** Compartments are separate parts of a container where things can be kept apart from others. In the vault, different owners' gold is kept in different compartments.

**cylinder (SIL-uhn-dur)** A cylinder is an enclosed shape with round ends and straight sides. The entrance to the gold vault is shaped like a cylinder.

**intercom (IN-tur-kahm)** An intercom is a system that allows a person to talk and listen to a person or people in another location. The vault surveillance team can speak to the guards through an intercom system.

**levers (LEV-urs)** Levers are bars or handles used to operate something on a machine. Levers are used to push bolts into holes to stop the cylinder's turning in the vault.

**pallets (PAL-its)** Pallets are wooden platforms used to support heavy things when they are being moved. Gold bars are moved on pallets into the gold vault.

**reinforced (ree-in-FORST)** Reinforced means something has been made stronger by adding more material. The concrete walls of the vault are reinforced with steel.

**surveillance (sur-VAY-luntz)** Surveillance is the act of watching closely. Secret agents kept suspected bomber Quazi Nafis under surveillance.

**trapezoid (TRAP-uh-zoid)** A trapezoid is a shape with four sides, two of which are parallel. The United States produces gold bars in the shape of a trapezoid.

**vault (VAWLT)** A vault is a room for keeping valuable items safe. Gold valued at $194 billion is stored in the gold vault at the Federal Reserve Bank of New York.

# TO LEARN MORE

## IN THE LIBRARY

Holub, Joan. *What Was the Gold Rush?* New York: Grosset & Dunlap, 2013.

Houghton, Gillian. *How Banks Work.* New York: PowerKids Press, 2009.

Orr, Tamra. *Coins and Other Currency: A Kid's Guide to Coin Collecting*. Newark, Delaware: Mitchell Lane Publishers, 2008.

## ON THE WEB

Visit our Web site for links about guarding the Federal Reserve Bank of New York: **childsworld.com/links**

*Note to Parents, Teachers, and Librarians: We routinely verify our Web links to make sure they are safe and active sites. So encourage your readers to check them out!*

## INDEX